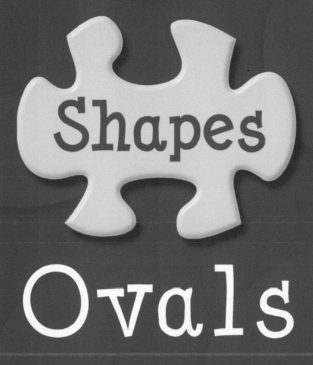

Shapes

Ovals

by Sarah L. Schuette

Reading Consultant:
Elena Bodrova, Ph.D., Senior Consultant,
Mid-continent Research for Education and Learning

A+
books

an imprint of Capstone Press
Mankato, Minnesota

A+ Books are published by Capstone Press,
1710 Roe Crest Drive, North Mankato, Minnesota 56003.
www.capstonepub.com

Library of Congress Cataloging-in-Publication Data
Schuette, Sarah L., 1976–
    Ovals / by Sarah L. Schuette.
    p.cm—(Shapes)
    Summary: Simple text, photographs, and illustrations show ovals in everyday objects and actions.
    Includes bibliographical references and index.
    ISBN-13: 978-0-7368-1461-4 (hardcover)   ISBN-10: 0-7368-1461-2 (hardcover)
    ISBN-13: 978-0-7368-5059-9 (softcover pbk.)   ISBN-10: 0-7368-5059-7 (softcover pbk.)
    I. Ovals—Juvenile literature. [1.Ovals.] Title.
QA483 .S38 2003
516'.5—dc21   2002000895

Created by the A+ Team

Sarah L. Schuette, editor; Heather Kindseth, art director and designer; Jason Knudson, designer
    and illustrator; Angi Gahler, illustrator; Gary Sundermeyer, photographer; Nancy White,
    photo stylist

Note to Parents, Teachers, and Librarians

The Shapes series uses color photographs and a nonfiction format to introduce children to the shapes around them. It is designed to be read aloud to a pre-reader or to be read independently by an early reader. The images help early readers and listeners understand the text and concepts discussed. The book encourages further learning by including the following sections: Table of Contents, Words to Know, Read More, Internet Sites, and Index. Early readers may need assistance using these features.

Printed in the United States   5685

Table of Contents

Oval shapes are round and long.

4

5

1

2

3

4

hen do the same with each space.

Space Notes

Line Notes

Turn to p. 39. Identify each note as a *line* or *space* note.

s. Together we call them the **GRAND STAFF**.

Musical notes are like letters of the alphabet. They spell out a song. Each oval note is worth a different number of beats. These beats are just like the beating of your heart.

Oval notes make up a song.

Did you ever notice that a zero is an oval? The poor zero does not count by itself. It counts only when it comes after a number from one to nine.

Ovals help to show your age.

Your whole body needs protection from the sun's rays. Even on cloudy days, rays from the sun can still be strong. Put on your sunglasses and sunscreen. Then have fun in the sun.

How many ovals are on this page?

Pictures sit in oval frames.

Oval rinks hold
hockey games.

Toy trains travel
on oval tracks.

Train tracks are highways for trains. Railroad cars travel along tracks to bring people and supplies to different places. An engineer drives a real train.

Oval crackers make tasty snacks.

Oval soap sits
in an oval dish.

Shoot this oval
if you wish.

No matter how you stretch or pull a rubber band, it will always come back to its original shape.

Oval platters are part of a set.

Is an oval part of the alphabet?

Make Oval People Prints

You will need

finger paint

paper

pens or markers

1 Dip your finger or thumb in the paint.

PAINT

2 Use your thumb to make prints all over the piece of paper. Let the paint dry.

3 Draw faces, legs, arms, hats, and other things on your fingerprints.

Words to Know

alphabet—all the letters of a language arranged in order; the English alphabet has 26 letters starting with the letter A and ending with the letter Z.

beat—the regular rhythm of a piece of music or your heart; each musical note is worth a different amount of beats; whole notes are ovals worth four beats.

note—a written symbol that stands for a musical sound

ray—a narrow beam of light; the sun gives off many rays of light; rays from the sun are very strong.

set—a group of things that go together; the objects in a set usually have the same color, shape, or look.

Read More

Burke, Jennifer S. Ovals. City Shapes. New York: Children's Press, 2000.

Court, Robert. Shapes. Chanhassen, Minn.: Child's World, 2002.

Pluckrose, Henry Arthur. What Shape Is It? Let's Explore. Milwaukee: Gareth Stevens, 2001.

Salzmann, Mary Elizabeth. Ovals. What Shape Is It? Edina, Minn.: Abdo, 2000.

Index